BIRDS OF PARADISE

BIRDS OF PARADISE

poems by

Christine Kitano

Lynx House Press
Spokane, Washington

ACKNOWLEDGMENTS

Grateful acknowledgment to the editors at the following publications in which these poems first appeared, some in different versions:

Arroyo Literary Review: "Last April in Syracuse" and "Magic Show"
Askew: "Luis's Hands"
Aspects of Robinson: Homage to Weldon Kees: "November Birthday"
Bear Flag Republic: Prose Poems and Poetics from California: "Birds of
    Paradise," "The Hour After," "Lost in the Move," "On Losing My Identity
    in Fourth-Grade Art Class," and "Oxnard"
Cloudbank: "Returning Home After My Father's Funeral, We Pass a Field of
    Sunflowers"
The Comstock Review: "Walking Past the House Where I Once Lived"
The Packinghouse Review: "Bile," "Dangerous," and "Three Pictures of My Mother"
Spillway: "Cooking Lesson"

I'd like to thank my teachers: Michael Burkard, Mary Karr, Chris Kennedy, Bruce Smith, and especially, Brooks Haxton. For the cover photo, thanks to Barbara Saito and the Kawaguchi family, Sudi, Lesley, and Joanne. Love and thanks to Derek McKown, best reader and best friend. And finally, thanks to Chizu Iiyama for her stories.

Copyright © 2011 Christine Kitano
Printed in America.

Author photo: Derek McKown
Cover & book design: Christine Holbert

FIRST EDITION

Library of Congress Cataloging-in-Publication Data
Kitano, Christine, 1985-
Birds of paradise : poems / by Christine Kitano.
    p. cm.
ISBN 978-0-89924-120-3 (alk. paper)
1. Japanese Americans—Poetry. I. Title.
PS3611.I8775B57 2011
811'.6—dc22
                          2011009705

TABLE OF CONTENTS

I

II

III

I

OMENS

When I was tall enough, my father
taught me to make Cream of Wheat.
After measuring the cups of milk and farina,
he'd stir the mixture with a long wooden spoon—
never metal—the scrape against the pot
shivered both our spines. It was bad luck,
he said, to cringe before breakfast.

The morning he returned home
after his first stroke, I made Cream of Wheat.
He was surprised how smooth
it was. I told him the key was patience,
stirring had to be even and rhythmic,
like the circular swish on a snare drum.
He was a musician so he understood.

The first New Year's Day after his death,
I made *mochi* by myself. He had told me
that the veil between the living and the dead
is permeable on the cusp between the years
and that gifts of sticky rice should always
be left out for the departed. I wasn't young
enough to expect much.

This morning, I find myself
picking anxiously at the dead skin
on my lips; the dry flakes fall
like candle wax shavings
into the hot steel pot—before
I throw it out, the cereal bubbles,
lit from below by foaming ghosts.

GUT STRINGS

Startled awake by a sound
at three in the morning
I think: someone is waiting
for me to die, to crack my bones
open in search of music.
In the next room, my cello groans,
the strings pull against
their iron screws. The strings
snap the wood and uncoil.
Maybe I should be reading more,
eating better. The cello's gut
strings are made from sheep
intestines; the guts are pulled
steaming from their still
pulsing bodies. To allow
the organs to cool risks
the honesty of the string.
But too many gut strings ring
false, something goes wrong
between the death and the uncoiling,
before the string is stretched
over the instrument's belly –
the animal's fat splits the gut fibers,
smearing the sound; or, spookily,
the dead fibers retain a sense
of the animal: the second smallest
sheep in the herd was afraid of heights,
and even dead, its guts still shrivel
with the ascent in pitch, the string
wilting, killing the sound.
Tonight, the dry air disagrees
with both me and my cello.

My hair rises and sparkles and I hear
another string snap, sharp
and sudden like the breaking
of bone, vibrations after
like a glow, an echo, like my pulse.

DANGEROUS

Like holding a glass of red wine
over a brand new white silk nightgown,
a chemise, the tag calls it.

I'm not beautiful enough to wear it. I'd fall
asleep and wake covered in blood—a blister
between my ribs would burst, or something deeper

inside, something too ugly to bear
being covered in English lace. I wore pretty things
as a child. My mother dressed me

every day, to make me
real. Without pretty clothes
I was a broken doll. Once, she ripped

a dress in two. It was pink, cotton, and soft,
and in a dry screech, gone, disintegrated
into thread, into dandelion dust.

That anger lingers in me now, when I tip
the wine glass over the new chemise,
and watch red ink blots

bloom and pool. My mother
said my face was stained
by the sun. She threatened to burn

the freckles off my cheeks and patch
the scars with make-up, promising
they'd heal, smooth and shiny,
a permanent mask.

LOST IN THE MOVE

Photograph: Ballet Recital, age, 6.
      The applause has stopped,
      the mothers and fathers have ushered
      their daughters home, draping crushed velvet coats
      over pink leotards. Waiting, alone
      under the empty lights, I crouch down
      to the stage and collect shed rose petals.
      My mother clicks the camera
      by accident, trying to wind the film.

Photograph: Aunt Chizu, age 22; Topaz Internment Camp, Utah;
July, 1944.
      Her smile is wide and sun-bright
      on the black & white film. She points
      to the laces of her saddle shoes.
            "Tar," she'd say, sixty years later, shaking
            her head, "it melted in the sun – sticking our soles
            to the ground." She'd smile, again,
            to herself and laugh. "Your father
            brought his trombone."

Photograph: Seventh Birthday.
      I pinch the pig tail
      of a large orange balloon,
      and smile despite the fear
      I feel, that at any moment
      the balloon will break free,
      slip away, disappear
      up a chimney of clouds.
      In the background, my father
      leans against the yellow porch swing
      and tips the lip of a glass tumbler, swallowing
      his medication with wine.

ON LOSING MY IDENTITY
IN FOURTH-GRADE ART CLASS

Mrs. DeHaven passed out sheets of paper and placed a coffee can filled with crayons in the center of each group of desks. We were drawing "self-portraits," she explained. The best artist would win a prize.

I was small and shy and when time came to color my hair, the black and brown were taken. If I pressed down hard above the forehead I thought, the purple would be dark enough.

I smeared a waxy bruise before the paper wrinkled, then tore, the desk's wooden grain a lightning bolt splitting the make-believe eyes.

BUCKET & NEEDLE

Mom brings Grandma back
from playing mahjong
with the Han sisters. She seems
smaller than she did last week
at the farmer's market,
when she taught me how
to inspect the chalk-white eyes
of fish and the lay of their silver scales.

She's quiet now
and I sit with her
by the stove. I offer
her my doll, but instead
she reaches for me,
begins to braid my hair.
Her cold hands smell
of fish and garlic.
When I try to pull away,
she clings tighter and whimpers.

Later in my room, Lizzie,
my imaginary twin, crawls out
from under the bed.
We play checkers.
I hear Mom on the phone,
telling that Grandma swallowed
a mahjong tile. Lizzie winks
and says she was there, the one
who tricked Grandma to think
the tile was a square of lime jello.
I forgive her only when
she sneaks to the kitchen,

past Grandma's hunched frame,
and back, two cookies in hand.

Grandma's singing in a language
I've never heard, a song
I don't know except
the Korean words
mool-tong and *bah-nil,*
bucket and needle.
It scares me
when Lizzie says this
is a song she knows.

BILE

My mother, after vomiting
into the sink in my grandmother's
bathroom, looks up to glare

at me. I feel the cold
brass doorknob against my cheek.
She's crying. I brace myself

against the door. "I wish
I were dead," she says.
"I'd kill myself right now,"

she points a shaking finger,
"if it weren't for you. Look
what I do for you. Look

at everything I do
for you. I have to stay
alive and suffer because of you."

The bathroom reeks
of bile. My new dress is streaked
with it. My mother cries

for her mother, calls out,
her crooked words Korean,
and cryptic as a spell.

BALLET, MUSIC, *IKEBANA*

At ballet class,
in my music lessons,
I believed my mother,
that I might be
someone else, with perfect
pitch, graceful, flawless;
but with flowers,
pushing wires
into tender green stalks,
weighing down stems
with stones so their arc
appeared natural,
what I lacked
was not the question.
I gave my mother
the blooming purple iris
leaning in a slow
adagio toward the moss
at its base, the leaves unfolded
like curled ribbon, as if
beauty happened
like this, by chance,
without me.

BLUE SKIES

All enemy aliens and Japanese-Americans in the western halves of
California, Oregon and Washington and in the southern half of Arizona
will be placed under rigid new curfew regulations Friday,
and any violators will be immediately punished.

—*The San Francisco News,* March 24, 1942

After Pearl Harbor, my aunt tells me
her boss at the Chinese bakery let her go
fifteen minutes early, just
in time to hurry home, seven rice cakes
tucked in her purse, before the curfew.
In the lobby of my grandfather's hotel,
she and her six sisters and brothers unwrapped
the sweets in mandated darkness and listened
to my father practice his trombone—
Dorsey's solos in *Blue Skies, Song of India*—
having lost their radio to the police,
he played from memory. Many years

later, listening to me at our piano,
my father pinched my earlobe, and told me
I should learn to play by heart. My mother says
he whispered to her, "She'll never be a musician."

The government would take my grandfather's
Nob Hill Hotel, and in the months leading
up to the relocation, the family lives
in darkness. My father's trombone, despite
the shut curtains, glints in an overflow
of moonlight, the sweet, muted tone
escaping concealment, drowning the wail

of a falsely triggered air raid siren.
He holds the trembling notes in the back
of his throat, as his sisters savor
their sticky cakes, making
the sweetness last.

THE HOUR AFTER

The doctor hands me a plastic drawstring bag. Inside are my father's khaki Dockers, his white undershirt, and a pair of brown socks, the elastic around the ankles pulled loose. His shoes are gone and so is the cash from his wallet.

I empty the bag onto the carpet in his bedroom. When he took me on the carousel at the Pier, he'd hug my waist so I wouldn't slip from my seat on the wooden white horse, my small hands clinging to its sleek mane. Every time the flushing horizon came around I would point, and he would look.

Inside the pocket of his pants I find a half-eaten chocolate bar, melted around the wrapper's torn edge. He always broke his candy in two, saving half for me when I came home from school. This half is mine. I peel back the melted paper and break off a square. The sugary syrup stings my back molar. When I breathe in, my head goes hollow.

BIRDS OF PARADISE

My father planted tomatoes under
his study window for concentration,
strawberries outside our bedrooms to favor
sweet dreams. The plaque in his garden hut
read: Your plants, your children.

When they bloomed, the rush
of white irises and morning glories
would encircle the house like a fog.
I played outside—cupped the canoe-shaped bract
of a Bird of Paradise in my hand and pretended
to be an African queen, the stunning orange
bird my companion, or Sleeping Beauty,
the flower's sharp stigma a poisoned spindle.

My father swam every day of summer.
I'd sit with my crayons and watch,
drawing pictures of him, of birds,
of squirrels shot dead with a pellet gun
before they tore the ripe buds from his plants.
I drew what I knew about the lives
of flowers, blooms diving out
from wrinkled shells, unfurling
thin petals—pale, wet butterflies.

He'd dive in, piercing the pool's calm
surface with his fingertips, spreading
his hard arms wide, a white spray
erupting into wings.
He swam with such power
I almost forgot who he was.

PICTURE OF MY FATHER AS A YOUNG MAN

He's just about to stand, left knee
to the grass, right foot extended,
ready to push his weight up.
His hands, large and sunlit, still
betray a tension around the knuckles,
a force that might form a fist.

Years later, after closing
his eyelids with a wet washcloth,
a nurse will struggle to free
the hospital sheet
from his stiffened grip.

But here he's in motion,
finding his rhythm.
Curls swept high by a wind.

1945: MY FATHER LEAVES
TOPAZ INTERNMENT CAMP, UTAH

At war's end, my father, nineteen,
rode the train from Salt Lake to Milwaukee
to take a job killing cows—for that one year
he stopped eating meat.

If you strike, he said, the hollow
between the animal's eyes, and if the ax is right,
the pain is quick. The cow's heavy collapse
the worst sound he'd remember.

When the families were herded
into trains with unknown destinations,
my grandmother dressed her children
in their best clothes, in case
they were being taken away to be shot.
She might have shrugged when she saw
the neighbors, dressed in rags
for the same uncertainty.

THREE PICTURES OF MY MOTHER

I. Backyard Photograph

Stuck on her hip
like a photographer's prop, I look
like a boy. Her thick, dark hair, longer
than I ever remember, falls over her shoulders
as if just loosed the second before
my father, his boyish gaze
seeing only her, clicks.

II. Tijuana, Mexico

My father guest lecturing in San Diego,
my mother hails a cab to Tijuana. She still looks
like a college student in her fringed denim,
the ribbons of her espadrilles looped
around her ankles like a ballet dancer's.
At six, I copy her every move, and sedulously buckle
sandal straps into place. I stay in her shadow
as she angles in and out of marketplace stalls,
strokes and snaps the leather belts, and dips
her fingers in a barrel of glass-beaded rosaries.
She picks one for each of us. I clutch
the tiny cross close when a group of girls
my age surrounds us, flip-flops slapping
concrete, singing "Chiclets! Chiclets!"
In a cantina, thick slatted shutters break
the afternoon sunlight into dusty beams.
My mother's face illuminated, she tips back
a glass of tequila and begins to cry.
Her tears catch the light like small, perfect beads.
Next to her, shaded, I kneel on the bar-stool.
Our eyes almost meet. She stares through me.
I sneak a half moon slice of lime into my mouth.

III. Surrender

Last summer, her thin wiry hair pulled
back, short meek wisps that frame
her yellowed forehead like broken threads,
she hides behind large oval sunglasses.
I'm leaving her. In the backyard, emptied
first of my father, now of me, she hangs our
white slips to dry. The narrow rectangles
balloon with wind.

DECEMBER 31, 1999

Tomorrow is bringing the end of the world
but we have come to clean
our new apartment. Buckets of bleach
and Lysol sanctify the space.

Sunlight streaks the bare
wooden floor. It is never winter
in California. I dust the window ledges
in my bedroom. Down the street,

from the donut shop, my father returns
with a pink boxful for breakfast.
We sit on the living-room floor, as if
for a picnic. In less than a year,

my father will die. In two years,
my mother will re-marry. Nobody gets
to say when the world will end.

The portable radio announces
that Y2K has arrived in China
and everything's fine.

CREATION MYTH

I. Water, 1900

My teenaged grandfather crouches
in a shadowed doorway
after his eldest brother's funeral, hand cupped
around his mouth, his habitual pose to hide
his cleft palate. He hears his mother say,
 "If any of my children had to die, why
couldn't it have been Motoji?"
Within a year he'll be gone,
finding work on a steamer, jumping
ship while docked in San Francisco.

II. Earth, 1914

A young woman stands ankle-deep
in a rice paddy. Having lost
her hair to an illness, she wears
a silk handkerchief, tied in a knot
at her throat. At twenty-four she is considered
unmarriable, weak and an old maid. A single
photograph is sent to America,
to a bachelor with a cleft palate. She can't hope
for more. At night, by firelight,
her father sharpens his old samurai sword.
She wonders how many men
he has killed, if any
blood lingers on the slim, handsome blade.

III. Air, 1969

My mother arrives from the sky,
her first trip on an airplane, flying
from Seoul to her new home. They stop

in Hawaii en route to Los Angeles.
She is sixteen. "It's true," she whispers
to her sleeping sister, peering out
the window over Honolulu,
"America is paradise." Because
of an ink smudge, her name, Choi,
is recorded as Chai.

IV. Fire, 2000

Skipping class to read under the bleachers,
I learn it wasn't the earthquake so much
as the fires that broke that city in 1906.
My grandfather could claim
his citizenship papers burned, was issued anew.

I am born of everybody's second choice.

The morning of my father's funeral,
the shower water goes cold when I look down
and see strands of my hair looped
around my ankles like thin, dark ribbons.
I remember sneaking into my grandmother's bedroom
to examine the row of foam wig-heads
on her dresser: five blank faces with eyes painted blue.

My father is ash when we throw
him overboard, white bits
of bone flecking the Pacific.

II

FORM

The night my father died
my mother dreamt of gray swallows,
my aunt of twelve black lilies,
my grandmother of her mother
in a white dress, ankle-deep in sand,
crying. I slept with the dog on the couch.
She pressed her prune nose into my palm.

That morning, for the first time
in my sixteen-year life, I touched
my father's stereo set, pushed play
on the tape deck. White noise hummed
out of the speakers, from which I tried
to recognize a voice. But no, and when
I drew the curtains open, the room filled
not with ash, but light.

MAGIC SHOW

The man on-stage slices open
a small lemon and from the yellow pulp
pulls the dollar bill, signed by my father
in red ink. The audience applauds and laughs
but I'm scared, terrified that my father has lost
control, given over power of himself
to this man in a black suit waving
white-gloved hands, much larger
than my father's. The next morning,
when I lift up the quilt on my father's bed,
I'm not surprised to find he's vanished,
and it's him, not the magician, I blame.
When the magician asked for a volunteer,
it was my father who raised his hand.

INSOMNIAC NOTEBOOK

When the sun fades, she steeps the bag of chamomile, stirs in honey
    and warm milk.
The voice on the meditation tape whispers, *Visualize the color red.*
So she tries. A crate of apples, a barn falling down. The rust red
    of her first car.
Then orange, and yellow, and so on until violet.
Violet: an umbrella opening in a dark rain. A wet road. A balloon
    she lost as a child, the small dark shape against the blue.
Streetlamps blink off. Night fades. Daylight is fuzzy at the window.
    Nausea.
The echo in her left ear, as if pressed to the cavity of a seashell.
    The taste of salt
in her throat. The body exhausted and shutting down. But sleep
    doesn't come.
Climbing every night the spiral stair toward sleep, she finds
    an open window
at the top, a dark violet sea spread below.
She blinks, and drowsiness passes like a missed wave.

A GIRL VISITS THE BEDSIDE OF A DYING MAN

He says he woke from anesthesia
out of a dream, a nightmare, breath
in short gasps. Now, he says, he's at the top
of a roller-coaster drop, and when the ride is over,
he'll be dead. Instead of reaching toward him,
her arm stiffens at her side. Are you listening?
His heart, once overfilled, is now
deflating, a submerged balloon with a slit
the thickness of an eyelash.
The descent, he says,
It isn't what you'd think. It's slow.
He lowers his eyelids, raises his arms in an arc
above his head, like a dancer,
and dies like that,
as if reaching, as if hopeful.

LUIS'S HANDS

Harbor Sushi; Riverside, California.

Watching him plunge
a glass into the hot rinse water
I was stunned to see
that his magnified hands
looked like two orange koi
swimming in and out
of the cup's mouth . . .
his fingers slithering
against its slippery walls.

His hands were bright red
when he pulled them
from the water and I
reached mine toward his.
He clapped his palms
over my knuckles. His hands
were hot, and though wet
with soap, I could feel
dry, scaly calluses beneath
the filmy exterior.
He smelled of the lemon
dish-soap our manager bought
in gallons and watered down
to last all year.
I asked him
why he was working here, and
he asked me the same—
we didn't meet each other's eyes
when we answered.

He unclasped his hands and
wiped them on my black apron,
leaving two wet hand prints
next to my pocket, heavy
with quarters. He slipped
his hands over the pocket
and lifted the bulging material
away from my thigh.
I turned to leave and
the apron fell back against me,
the coins rattling
against my leg.
That night,
when I undressed,
I found an amber bruise
on my thigh. I pressed
my dry fingers against it
and went to bed thinking
of Luis, the muted smell
of lemon still on my hand.

JULY 4TH

Fresh from divorce, an old friend
visits. She asks my husband
about his first wife, first
as if second were second-best.
She asks if loving someone
ever stops. He shrugs. Maybe.

I know his first wife cooked well,
was good at pairing meals with wine.
I know she wore cashmere sweaters
and boutique underwear.

After dinner, I help my friend
make up the camp bed. She pulls
the pillow over her body like a shield.

Later, in our bed, I try to fall asleep
by matching my breaths to his, like a child
learning to swim. Outside it begins to rain,
and wet maple leaves plaster themselves
to the bedroom window. When finally
I pull the sheets over my head, I take a deep,
long breath. My chest fills—a diver going under.

UNTWINNED

One in eight
of us begins as a twin.
When mine died,
I ate her.

At night, I whisper
bedtime stories.
She likes the Greek myths,
the flame-breathing chimera
that swallows its own throat,
the twins on white steeds.

I look for her
in the polished chrome
of the playground slide,
or in the hand-mirror I keep
under my pillow. When I can't
sleep, I practice fitting my fist
into my mouth. It helps me
to feel whole.

WIND

Outside, in the crosswalk,
a strong wind pushed me forward
so I missed a speeding car
by a foot. Splayed on the asphalt,
I rolled over, tipped my head
to the sky, and spotted, in a plum tree,
heavy with overripe fruit,
a crimson wisp of smoke,
whipped away by the wind.

DROWNING

The less of me to love,
the better, and so I was taught
to always leave half my portion
uneaten. I tried to disappear,
invisibility the best defense against
my mother's anger. I pinned my hair
across my eyes like a fence,
pulled the drawstring
hood of my sweatshirt
tight against my throat.
Not knowing its real purpose,
I sneaked a scoop of vanishing cream
from the jar on her dresser
and smeared it on my skin
before bed. I fell asleep
holding my breath,
praying that it would work,
that I might vanish
in my sleep, but instead
dreamed of drowning, face to face,
my mother the one
holding us both under.

WAITING AT THE LAUNDROMAT

Propped on a folding table,
I relax against the window's warm glass,
stare at the porthole of the washing machine
across the aisle. Water glides in, explodes
into foam. A red t-shirt darkens.
Glycerine streaks slide down the glass
the way Mr. Pyle's fingers must have
when he drove his Buick off the bridge.
The police when they found him, still strapped
in his seat belt, called my grandmother,
his landlord and only known contact.

Quarters clamor from the change machine
by the door. Outside, it's fifteen degrees
but inside this small, dryer-warmed room,
I feel a thaw in my bones. Lucky,
is what my grandmother said,
of Mr. Pyle's death. That he didn't die alone
in bed, undiscovered for a week.
In his apartment, she found
a locked safe, too heavy to lift.
A box like that, she thought, must
be filled with hundred-dollar bills
in neat stacks, or diamonds wrapped in velvet.
She had the locksmith spring the iron door free,
and found daily racing forms,
an archive of years' unrewarded hunches.

Old clothes swirl in soap and water.
Why didn't Mr. Pyle unbuckle
his seat-belt, try to escape—was it shock,
or did he believe this to be his luck,

his small reward? Why smash the window,
only to keep swimming?
I, too, might close my eyes and wait.

COMMUNITY POOL

Why can't I stop
watching this girl, pale blue
bikini suit, no more than nine,
slinging the whip

of her wet braid? I was her
age once. I had control
as I edged toward blossom.

But when my body split
from its childhood skin,
I opened like a parachute,
jerked upward with a bitter kiss
before the fall.

INSOMNIAC'S *ARS POETICA*

> . . . every thing in the dim light is beautiful,
> The wildest and bloodiest is over, and all is peace.
> Peace is always beautiful,
> The myth of heaven indicates peace and night.
>
> —*Walt Whitman,* "The Sleepers"

Where do they come from,
these nightmares that take
reign, pry my eyelids open,
wrench me awake, the elastic blue
strap of my nightgown
tangled with my tongue.

At night, the air is like chalk
in my throat. I suck on blister-
sized lozenges, seesaw side-
to-side under a sticky quilt, and wait
for two a.m. when I forfeit
the cunning sheets.

I cannot see the moon
from my bedroom window, but
the streetlamp just outside
is near enough. Those arms
of light. Would they be cool
or warm? I think it would depend
on the temperature of the night,
the temperament of the patient.
This nightly ritual—

Reaching out to the glowing
profluence of light, dreams slipping
between the glare's ordered particles—
part magic-trick, part survival.

AFTER THE SHOW

The magician's white-gloved hands flap like dove wings.
From the well of his hat he pulls a small, white rabbit,
      a red ribbon drooping from its neck.
From my seat in the audience, it might look like blood.
This must be what he intends.

Outside, the road home wavers like a rope.
Wet with moonlight, it might be a river.
Small white clematis blooms glow like stars
      lining this road of night.
From where I stand, it might be vanishing.

INSOMNIAC'S BEST NIGHTMARE

To ward off nightmares
I keep a rabbit's foot
in the shoebox under the bed,
also an apple's shriveled
core, and a wet balloon.

Past midnight
I watch infomercials,
and at sunrise
pay the gas bill.

Later, in a fitful sleep,
I chase my father. I find him
hiding, his slight body crouching
beneath a sunflower's thick stalk,
yellow petals shading his face
like a hat. My mother wipes her hands
on her blue apron and pulls the tail
of a cat, stiff and greasy,
from the front pocket. A tug
on my collar pulls me up,

Yanks me awake.
I yawn wide, my jaw clicks.
The sky is still black—not with night,
but crows.

III

ICHINOSAKA RIVER; YAMAGUCHI, JAPAN

Late April, early evening.
Darkness settles
over warm, lamp-lit air.
Paper lanterns rustle
against cherry blossom leaves.

Women gossip and fill
wooden cups at the flickering
water. Koi, with orange
and white scales, black
spots I mistake for eyes,
shimmer past.

Tangerine pulp beneath
my fingernails, broken
tangerine skins at my feet.
A boy clasping a glass jar
chases swarms
of fireflies. Down
the bank, alone
against the outline
of the moon,
and old man's
silhouette fades.

FINDING THE FAMILY TREE

I fell asleep on the sand.
It was like a black & white photograph.
I didn't hear the surf.
I woke up in a bed of waves.

I was in line for the Ferris wheel.
My sandaled toes were sticky with salt.
The carousel ponies grinned fiercely.
When I touched a child's braid, she cried.
My startled shadow cut in line and went up alone.

"They will be put to shame who are treacherous
without excuse," warns my schizophrenic brother, leaving
messages on the phone every evening. His end clicks
as soon as I pick up. He thinks I'm someone else.

Running the ring-toss stand at night,
I watch girls from school with long hair
loop arms with their boyfriends, throw
their heads back and laugh.
I present them with large stuffed bears.
They pretend not to know me.

Home from work I watch old movies.
Actors with flat, gray faces.
In the bathroom mirror, under the humming
fluorescent light, behind the face
of my dead sister, I am sad, again
        to find myself.

RICH COUSIN GETTING MARRIED

The mailbox empty
but for a check from my mother
and instructions to buy a nice dress
for a cousin's wedding.
There should be a private room
for girls like me, searching
out that dress to wear
like a disguise, altering
limp bodies under fluorescent light.
In the mirror, hair undone,
make-up smeared on the pastel satin
zipped up askew: please transform me.
But when I step out of the fitting stall,
the other women avoid my eyes.
Maybe I should be the one
in law school, marrying an engineer,
buying a starter-house with loft
and two-car garage.
Back home, the gas bill waits,
the coffee pot leaks, dishes soak,
unwashed. I just want a place
to warm my feet: hot shower,
heat turned on full blast
because it's cold outside,
too cold for snow.

OXNARD, CALIFORNIA

At the entrance to the lobby
of the Casa Sirena Hotel,
dressed in pale blue overalls,
pink blouse with ribbons tied
in neat bows across the collar,
white lace-trimmed socks,
and new sneakers,
at three-years old, I feel
a rubber toe catch
on the checkered carpet,
and when I fall
face forward onto the track
of the sliding glass door,
my forehead splits open
like a baked potato.

In my mother's lap
on the way to be stitched,
the taxi's black leather
collects the day's heat
and when I reach down
with a sunburned hand,
my fingers stick
to the melting duct-tape
on a tear in the seat.
My mother is crying,
but I'm silent, wanting
to remember how
this feels, the stickiness
of the leather,
the tape, my blood,
and my mother's
sweaty skin against mine.

PERSEPHONE ACCUSES HER MOTHER

We're not supposed to know
the endings to our stories, but
that night I woke early
from a dream: I was only
a child, and you had stolen
the pomegranate from
my brown bag lunch.

I rolled over, reaching for
you but my arms grabbed
at nothing and I knew you
were gone. And it was because
you left after I had fallen
asleep and before I had
the chance to wake that
I took the kitchen scissors,
stared at myself hard
in the mirror and cut
off the length of my hair.
The dry strands fell
across my pale toes
and scattered like pine needles
on the cold tile floor.

Did you kiss my cheek
before you left? Or did
you know the faintness
of such a farewell
would be illuminated
by the glare of the moon
on your back—so bright
and so heavy?

RETURNING HOME AFTER MY FATHER'S FUNERAL, WE PASS A FIELD OF SUNFLOWERS

Heads bowed,
      dry corn-hued petals
angled at the sagging sun—
      their black faces follow
the light. If my father were
      a sunflower, swiveling his neck
to bask in my mother's smile,
      I was a seed, nestled in his cheek.
But now, my mother's spirit burns
      too brightly. And I, no more
than a spent shell, a tear-shaped
      drop of shell-meat, crawl
through a beam of dead light
      toward an invisible horizon.

MEDEA WRITES TO JASON

The photo on the back of the alumni newsletter: you,
       your new wife, posed in perfect handstands at the base
of the crumbling Acropolis. This, your consequent happiness—
district manager, vacations in Europe, a son on the way.

In my flower shop, I am greeted every morning
       by the faces of marigolds, violets, roses—
I guard their last hours, arrange them in vases,
       so they can wither and dry in pleasing posture.
The cleaner the cut, the longer they will keep.

My feet ache. I have been practicing cartwheels
       up and down the hallway for the past hour.
I will stand on my hands too, wingless,
       to defy the gravity of my divine weight
          in the face of a greater ruin.

COOKING LESSON

Hands only,
my grandmother instructs,
and thrusts hers, rivered
with purple veins—confident
only when cooking—into
the bowl of *jang-jorim,* kneading
the pepper and garlic
with the thread-thin strands of beef,
and tells me in Korea garlic bulbs
are large as fists, which sounds to me
like an image from a child's story
as I stand behind her, looking
at my hands, holding a wooden spoon
like a wand, trying to memorize the steps,
to learn a memory secondhand.

MOTHER

Teaching me at six to sew, my mother tells me no, not too much thread. Each thumb's length I spool out is one hundred steps I will move away from her when I marry. I love my mother, I want to be near her. I mend socks with a thread the length of a mouse-tail.

Even so, when she says no one else will ever love me, I tie one end of the thread to the kitchen doorknob and, holding the spool above my head, run outside and down the street, the wooden knob spinning in my hand. She sits still. I come home holding a cocoon of knotted thread to my chest. She calls me cruel. She cries.

I try to comfort her. I say I'd shave the hair from my head and tie the strands to make the thread to sew my wedding dress. I imagine finding the dress ripped at the seams. I scream and a voice echoes back, laughing. My mother tells me: You'd be ugly, bald.

LAST APRIL IN SYRACUSE

after Hayden Carruth

Spring-like weather, though it's still
April, early, it seems, too soon for this.
Where we live, it could be snowing.
And yet, the sugar maple, the other day only
an awkward brown skeleton, brushes its green
leaves against our third-story window,
and the pear trees bordering the streets
have popcorned into bloom. You say
this year's pollen count is higher than ever,
and maybe that's enough to account
for the sweat in my eyes as we box
the few belongings that can't be replaced:
books, mostly, but also your brother's
army jacket, my father's waffle iron,
the broken things we can't yet give up.

Sometime in October, overnight
the sugar maple outside
this window will redden, a shock
to the new tenants, perhaps new
to each other too, who will here learn
five different types of snow,
the names of their trees,
and one night will wake in bed,
face to face, amazed. And gently,
it will begin to rain.

COOKING AT NIGHT

In our small apartment
the kitchen opens into
the bedroom, but
3 am is so cold after hours
sleepless, reading recipes
on the net, and I had
to make spring rolls.
When you growled
at the crackle of oil,
the faucet squeak,
I felt better, pulling
you back from the edge
of sleep. My sleeplessness
is my fault. But I blame
you when you leave me
every night. And the warmth
of the steam, the sheer heat
from the oven is a comfort.
In the years ahead,
you will leave me.
And I'll spend every night
like this, writing to someone
who sleeps in another world.

NOVEMBER BIRTHDAY

The family piles heavy coats
at the entrance to the Chinese restaurant.
Grandmother is turning 88.
Seated at the large round table, she feels
the small warmth of a child against her shins.
Her youngest grandchildren, under the table,
swap fortune cookies before dinner.
One is not old as long as he is seeking something,
they read aloud. She remembers
her baby brother, 76 when he died,
and on that night, even before she knew,
she dreamed of him as a child. He was crying,
the two of them on a boat on a wide black sea.
She knows it would sound silly to tell
the fortune she knows: everything withers.
Cake arrives from the local bakery,
balloons bob like nodding ghosts,
walls patched with old photographs, the outlines
of friends, blurred in black and white.
From under the table, a sticky hand
pulls her down, and she's back at sea,
her arms full with the crying child.
They sway with the boat's steady heave.

WALKING PAST THE HOUSE WHERE I ONCE LIVED

I remember the bird the summer
I was seven, its gray-blue wing
grazing the side of my cheek
after it flew through the kitchen window.

Spoon in hand, I sat
unfazed as my mother pulled
a dishtowel over her head,
screamed and smashed the bird

with a frying pan. Rubbing
my right cheek, I insisted
on a funeral. In the back yard,
wearing my Christmas mittens,

I carried the corpse. According
to my father's Audubon guide,
it was an oak titmouse, also known
as the plain titmouse,

Baeolophus inornatus
of the Chickadee family.
Plain gray above, paler gray below;
crest gray.

Plain, gray, and though I didn't
know Latin then, still could guess
what *inornatus* might mean. I imagined
it was the type of bird I would be.

Plain gray Christine, also known as
the plain daughter, *Filia inornata*
of the Kitano family. Plain gray
above, paler gray below; crest gray.

Tail average. Acrobatic feeder; eats
nuts, seeds, grilled cheese.
Under "voice," the guide listed the words
see-dee-dee. See-dee-dee, I whispered,

tucked the plain gray bird
into the earth. My mother screeched
from the kitchen window, It's dirty!
See-dee-dee, I sang back, See-dee-dee.